My Alabaster Box

by

Linda Mura

authorHOUSE®

AuthorHouse™
1663 Liberty Drive, Suite 200
Bloomington, IN 47403
www.authorhouse.com
Phone: 1-800-839-8640

First published by AuthorHouse 3/18/2008

ISBN: 978-1-4343-4227-0 (sc)

Library of Congress Control Number: 2007908845

Printed in the United States of America
Bloomington, Indiana

This book is printed on acid-free paper.

Scripture quotations (NIV) are taken from the new international version.

Picture of alabaster box was done by Aimee Photography.

Acknowledgments

To my children, Michele, Brian and Daniel, for forgiving me and loving me even though I failed you. Thank you for your grace. You are three precious gifts that God has given me and I love you.

To all the women that God has placed in my life over the years that have loved me enough to speak truth even when I didn't want to hear it and walked along side of me to show me Jesus when I needed it most. You are too numerous to mention. I love you all.

Thank you, Julie for taking time out of your busy schedule to edit the book for me. You're great.

Forward

Lord, what do you want me to hear this morning? Why am I here?

You're here because I love you! I have always loved you even when you didn't think you were worthy. The sounds you hear and the colors you see is a pallet I painted for you to enjoy. Your life is in my hands. Will you trust me?

Crawl into my lap and I'll hold you for awhile, but then you have to go, for I have work for you to do. Love them; let them see Jesus in you. Touch them with a heart of compassion. There are many to reach. Come to me, listen to what I say. You don't walk alone; there will be others to help you.

You are my daughter; each morning is a new day. Come spend them with me and I will guide your steps. I have given you wisdom and understanding. Love them well; those I put in your care.

Don't be afraid I have equipped you with all you need. I am always here; all you have to do is call on me. Just reach out your hand and your heart. We'll do it together.

All is Not Lost

I had no idea while attending a prayer retreat for women, that the Holy Spirit was about to begin a work in my life and I would soon come to realize that all my years of pain and suffering would be revealed to me as a refining process to give my life purpose and meaning.

For years I beat myself up because of poor relationships, a lack of caring for myself, several failed marriages, and wondered what God could possibly want with me. Anything I had ever tried seemed to fail. While gathering with friends one evening to pray, a friend leaned over to me and whispered in my ear, "I'm the woman at the well." What a relief! Someone I respected and thought of as a godly woman was just like me. Through that simple statement God began to set me free. If he could use her life he could surely use mine. He did want me! He had a purpose for my life. Jeremiah 29:11 NIV says, "For I know the plans I have for you," declares the Lord, "plans to prosper you and not to harm you, plans to give you hope and a future."

God takes our failures and mistakes, our pain and our suffering, and uses them to help others. He uses people who think they are rejects to show others the love of Christ. He's shown me that I have worth and value and it comes from Him, not my spouse, not my children, but Jesus. Where other people see failure, God sees a disciple. From the wisdom of my pain and trials, he has allowed me to plant seeds and help others. I can share with younger women, while they are in the spring of their life to discover their potential and who they are.

God is all I need. When I apply the blood of Jesus to my life; when I praise the Lord; when I stand firm and say I am His; as I expose the darkness inside me to the light and get honest about who I am and what I've done, I walk free of shame and torment. Ephesians 5:13-14 "But everything exposed by the light becomes visible, for it is light that makes everything visible."

If I do these things does it mean that my life is free of trouble? On the contrary! The attacks of the enemy sometimes seem even greater than before. My marriage faces conflict, my children live their own lives; I struggle with temptation; the closer I draw to God the more the spiritual warfare. I do know that as long as I walk with God and look up and not at the mess around me, I can get through anything. God seems to reach down into the mess and make miracles. I live in faith knowing that he takes what I see as hopeless and gives me hope.

We need to call forth the things of God as though they were and have faith. He works through my faith. Hebrews 11:1 "Now faith is being sure of what we hope for and certain of what we do not see."

I Peter 1:8-9 "Though you have not seen Him, you love Him; and even though you do not see Him now, you believe in Him and are filled with an inexpressible and glorious joy, for you are receiving the goal of your faith, the salvation of your souls."

When you think your marriage is less than perfect, your children are on drugs, your past is too horrible for anyone to see, remember that when we stand naked and unashamed in front of the Lord, we all look the same. Give your spouse, your children, your life to God for none of it belongs to you anyway; it's a gift from Him. Jesus can reach down in the depths of your despair and heal your marriage, save your children, and give you purpose. All he requires from you is your love and faithfulness. Matthew 7:33 "But seek ye first the Kingdom of God and His righteousness, and all these things will be given to you as well."

When the pain is strongest, when you think you can't go another step, don't give up. Wherever you are, Jesus will meet you there. Don't listen to the lies of the enemy. We walk through our lives with pain and suffering and each time we work through the pain and feel it, healing comes. When things seem the worst, Jesus is getting ready to use you; he's getting ready to birth a miracle in your life; he's refining you. Don't run to a place of comfort away from the Lord; run into your Father's loving arms; take hold of his hand and let him lead you through the turmoil. Look at what it cost Jesus to buy us the ability to change.

Each time you move through the pain you peel off a layer. When the pain comes again and you face it, another layer drops off (it's the 99 year plan), and then one day you will look into God's face and know he has refined you into pure gold. Pain is a refining process, sometimes a walk in the furnace.

You say, "I can't do this. My husband is not the person I married; my children are lost; you don't know what I have to live with." You're right, I don't, but when our doors close to the outside world we all deal with something. You can't fix it, but God is in the fixing business. He knows what goes on behind those doors. More than anything God wants **YOU**; he'll take care of the rest. Matthew 6:32-33 "Your heavenly father already knows perfectly well what you need and he will give it to you if you give him first place in your life and live as he wants you to." He will give you the desires of your heart when you delight in Him. Hebrews 4:13 "Nothing in all creation is hidden from God's sight. Everything is uncovered and lay bare before the eyes of him to whom we must give account."

Prayer is a powerful tool because when we pray, we wage war on the devil. So pray, lift your voice to the heavens and keep looking up, stay in a prayerful attitude, wage war on your enemy Satan. Recruit the heavenly saints to fight for you. You may not see them, but they are there with their swords drawn to protect you. I know my prayers for the salvation of my family and friends are honored by God as I wage spiritual warfare on their behalf. I will stand in the gap and plead the blood of Jesus over them. To believe this promise I had to know the One who made it by reading his Word and I had to learn to pray.

Does life always turn out the way we want it to? No. I don't have all the answers, but God has given me promises in his word and I stand on them. I will keep my eyes on Jesus and continue to praise him and give thanks to him for his faithfulness. I will depend upon the supernatural resources of God, which enable me to live the supernatural life, regardless of my circumstances. I will put my complete trust in him, for I am his child, and he cares for me. I will rest in his unfailing love and he will take care of everything that concerns me. I believe Romans 8:26-28 "In the same way, the Spirit helps us in our weakness. When we do not know what we ought to pray for, the Spirit himself intercedes for us with groans that words cannot express. And he who searches our hearts knows the mind of the Spirit, because the Spirit intercedes for the saints in accordance with God's will. And we know that in all things God works to the good of those who have been called according to his purpose."

I will take my disappointments and losses to him who loves me and rest in his arms and use the wisdom of my pain and sorrow to show others Jesus. When I stand before him, when my days are through, when he looks in my face, I want to hear "Well done my good and faithful servant."

YOU SEE NO MATTER HOW MY LIFE TURNS OUT, NO MATTER WHAT….ALL IS NOT LOST… HE HAS CHANGED ME…HE'S MADE ME WHOLE…SO HOWEVER THE STORY ENDS, I WIN!!!

"Even as Sarah obeyed Abraham, calling him lord; whose daughters ye are, as long as ye do well, and are not afraid with any amazement." 1 Peter 3:6

I am a masterpiece painted by a loving father with gifts that are unique to only me and by his hand I have changed from a reject to a miracle to serve Him and show His love to others in pain. My true beauty lies within my heart and glows from the inside out to shine so others can see I belong to God, I am His. I am Sarah's daughter.

"And the Lord visited Sarah as he had said, and the Lord did unto Sarah as he had spoken. For Sarah conceived, and bore Abraham a son in his old age, at the set time of which God had spoken to him." Genesis 21:1-2

There is nothing you can do to change where you've been or the mistakes you have made. Look over your past not with regret but with the knowledge that Jesus was with you carrying you and then look to the future with promise and know that he walks with you and that your children will come to a place where they will know him too. He has given you wisdom, discernment and the gift of encouragement; take these gifts and help the ones in the spring of their life to see Him and know that he is Lord. He has given you purpose, look forward, plant seeds, shine with the love of your father.

"..but those who hope in the Lord will renew their strength. They will soar on wings like eagles; they will run and not grow weary, they will walk and not faint."

You are an eagle.....SOAR, FEEL THE WIND IN YOUR FACE....SPREAD YOUR WINGS.....GLIDE ON THE WIND.....HEAR GOD'S WHISPER...AND KNOW...

YOU ARE MAGNIFICENT....YOU ARE AWESOME...YOU ARE GOOD ENOUGH...YOU ARE EVERYTHING BEAUTIFUL...YOU ARE UNIQUE...GOD'S CREATION.....A CHILD OF THE KING...AND SO MUCH MORE.....

"I, the Lord, have called you in righteousness; I will take hold of your hand. I will keep you and will make you to be a covenant for the people and a light for the Gentiles."
Isaiah 42:6

Jesus will give you peace and it will surround you like a mighty river; as his peace is within you share his love with others, show them by your life what he has done for you.

"…Fear not for I have redeemed you; I have summoned you by name; you are mine." Isaiah 43:1b

Jesus knows you inside out and he will protect you. Stand on the foundation of the cross. Cling to Jesus and when you feel like there is nothing left to hang on to, he will give you peace in the midst of confusion.

"For I know the plans I have for you, declares the Lord, plans to prosper you and not to harm you, plans to give you hope and a future. Then you will call upon me and come and pray to me and I will listen to you. You will see me and find me when you seek me with all your heart. I will be found by you, declares the Lord, and will bring you back from captivity."
Jeremiah 29:11-14

Jesus has a plan and a purpose for your life and in due season he will reveal it to you; lift your hands, praise his name and the words of the Lord will flow from your mouth. You are the righteousness of God, his daughter in whom he is well pleased. Your life will shine like a light in the darkness, your love for him will radiate from your face. The anointing will flow and wisdom and knowledge will be yours. He has given you many gifts; step into the river's flow, receive all he has for you for the mighty hand of God is upon you. Step out in boldness for he will cover you. Jesus has his arms around you; rest in them. Go forth today and use the gifts he gave you to glorify him. Feed his sheep, show them what he has done for you and let the love of Christ shine. Touch lives with the love of Christ and behold miracles and be forever thankful in your heart.

"You are my witness, declares the Lord, and my servant whom I have chosen." Isaiah 43:10

You are his daughter and he loves you; many will come your way and they will never leave the same. They will come with a heart of stone and will leave with a heart for Jesus. You have a compassionate heart and a willingness to serve others. He will send them and you will love them with the love of the Lord. He will never leave you nor forsake you. You belong to him. Let his light shine and he will cover you with his love and his blood. He has made a covenant with you. You are his daughter.

"Love is patient, love is kind. It does not envy, it does not boast, it is not proud. It is not rude, it is not self-seeking, it is not easily angered, it keeps no record of wrongs. Love does not delight in evil but rejoices with the truth. It always protects, always trusts, always hopes, always perseveres. Love never fails." I Corinthians 13:4-8

Jesus has given you love, more than anything walk in it. He has raised you up, you are his daughter, walk upright and confident that he is the Lord your God who moves heaven and earth. If he can do these things, how much more can he do for you because you love Him? He will move your mountain. Walk in love with everyone you see. Show them the love of Christ. He has come to give you life and life more abundantly; do not fear for he has a purpose for you, you are his daughter and he loves you. Show them love, wipe their tears away and show them he is the answer. Love your husband with the love Jesus has shown you and he will change your husband's heart. Wherever your feet are planted he will give you that place. Let His light shine from your face for he is the great I AM and he loves you.

"Consider it pure joy, my brothers, whenever you face trials of many kinds, because you know that the testing of your faith develops perseverance. Perseverance must finish its work so that you may be mature and complete, not lacking anything. If any of you lacks wisdom, he should ask God who gives generously to all without finding fault, and it will be given to him." James 1:2-5

Walk with Jesus and in your trials he will lift you up. He has given you gifts of wisdom, discernment and understanding; do not grow faint for he is always with you. He will keep his promises and when you hear his voice he speaks the truth. In all your ways honor him; when you speak his name (Jesus) people will see him in your face and life. You are his daughter full of the love of Christ. He will never forsake you or leave you. Do not worry for Jesus will supply your every need. If you walk in faith with a love of Christ that is beyond human understanding your heart will fill up with the love for him and his truth will flow from your lips. It is written.

"…….My grace is sufficient for you, for my power is made perfect in weakness…" 2 Corinthians 12:9

Jesus has wiped your slate clean, tomorrow is a new day, live in his presence and Satan is weak. Love him with your whole being; know that he is the Lord your God and that nothing is impossible if you only believe. Step out in faith and know that even though you cannot see him with your eyes, you can feel his presence through the eyes of your heart.

"Commit to the Lord whatever you do, and your plans will succeed." Proverbs 16:3

Jesus, I come to you today and ask for forgiveness of my sins, that my mind and body are full of the Holy Spirit down to the marrow of my bones. Bless me that I might have the character of God. Bless those I counsel Lord and touch their lives that they might know the depth of your love. Be with them and give them strength and be with their husbands and children that they might come out of bondage and love you. I pray that my husband will breathe in the wonder of you until you are always on his mind and in his heart. Widen the door for men that they will come by the hundreds to get to know you. Rise up the men in the church that they will become the spiritual heads of their homes. Lord let me be love today.

"The lips of the righteous nourish many, but fools die for lack of judgment." Proverbs 10: 21

Lord, let your blood cover me and protect me from the enemy. Fill me up with your Holy Spirit and give me wisdom and discernment. Forgive me for any unkindness that might have come from my mouth today. I pray that you encamp your angels around me. Lord, begin to do a work in me until I'm uncomfortable with any evil that tries to be a part of my life. I pray that my mind and heart belong to you. Watch over my children and bring them to full repentance and salvation in you. Encamp your angels around my home Lord and keep my family from evil. Let me see what a lavish of blessing would look like in my life and how it would change me for your glory. I pray for the people that I work with that your Holy Spirit will move in their hearts that they might come to know you.

"When pride comes, then comes disgrace, but with humility comes wisdom." Proverbs 11:2

Humble yourself in his presence, bless as you have been blessed; give as it has been given to you, for the Lord your God has set you free.

"The Lord will keep you from all harm—he will watch over your life; the Lord will watch over your coming and going both now and forever." Psalm 121:7-8

Jesus is more powerful than the enemy. Reach up and grab onto His hand and love Him with all your heart. The enemy can never win if you stand firm and hold on to Him. He loves you for you are his daughter.

"He reached down from on high and took hold of me; he drew me out of deep waters." Psalm 18:16

How I've missed you…It's so wonderful to sit at your feet once again, to open up the Bible and find you there speaking to me, giving me promises. I am so full of your Holy Spirit that I feel like I'm bursting with joy. I can't wait to get up in the morning and spend time with you. I am amazed at how staying in your presence changes my attitude and how your joy surrounds me. I am so thankful for the church and the Word of God. Love rises up in my heart and overflows. Thank you for reviving my heart, for renewing my soul, for touching me. You are my best friend and I love you with all my heart. Thank you for loving me and setting me free.

"But let all who take refuge in you be glad; let them ever sing for joy. Spread your protection over them, that those who love your name may rejoice in you. For surely, O Lord, you bless the righteous; you surround them with your favor as with a shield." Psalm 5:11-12

He will protect you, do not grow faint for the enemy will overtake you in your weakness, no matter what your circumstances, keep your eyes on Jesus for he is your Father, the one who holds you up and sets you free. Love him more than any living thing and his love will shine in your face and your life will reflect his love.

"But his delight is in the law of the Lord, and on his law he meditates day and night. He is like a tree planted by streams of water, which yields its fruit in season and whose leaf does not wither. Whatever he does prospers." Psalm 1:2-3

I come to you today Lord to renew my heart to begin a journey of renewed friendship with you. I have been too busy serving you. I want to sit with you, to hold your hand, to renew that friendship and closeness I had with you so long ago. Lord I want to get so close to you that I feel your breath on my neck. Please forgive me Lord that I've put other things before you. Revive my heart, my life. I don't want to live a mediocre life anymore; I want to live a life full of love for you. I want to honor you in everything I do. I want my life to have meaning for you Lord. I want to bear fruit so that my basket isn't only full but that it overflows and touches other lives. Lord let the people you bring into my life grow in you so that they touch others. I don't want it to stop with me. I want to be holy, Lord, to live a holy life, to be a vessel for you. Help me to be the servant you have called me to be, a woman of God. Use me Lord that I might show others the love of Christ. I love you Lord.

"A wife of noble character who can find? She is worth far more than rubies." Proverbs 31:10

Your husband wants to be big in your eyes, edify him and lift him up and he will become what he sees in your eyes. He needs to feel the love of the Holy Spirit and see what God can do for him. Love him as Christ loves you with an unconditional love. Step aside so that he might see the miracles as you see them and his heart will be totally changed. You are not your husband's Holy Spirit, let Jesus do His job. Your husband will come to a place where he loves Jesus with an unfailing love. God has called you to be a woman of excellence, don't settle for anything less. Sometimes this means humbling yourself and stepping aside so your husband may shine. You came out of the darkness and into the light; you are a beacon on a hill, a lighthouse for many. Love your husband, lift him up, be love to him. When his heart is fully God's you will have what you seek.

"Forget the former things; do not dwell on the past. See, I am doing a new thing! Now it springs up; do you not perceive it? I am making a way in the desert and streams in the wasteland." Isaiah 43:18-19

I'm so grateful, Father, that you rescued me from my past, that when the devil tries to remind me, I can give those thoughts to you and if necessary ask forgiveness. I wake up every morning looking for the new thing that you are about to do. I am so grateful that you go before me. As I look ahead, I can see streams of living water flowing through my life and where there was once sadness and pain, you placed the joy and peace of the Holy Spirit within me. Thank you for making me a new thing, for washing me white as snow. I will do my best to remember when the hard times come that you made me new and I have nothing to fear.

"...you whom I have upheld since you were conceived, and have carried since your birth. Even to your old age and gray hairs I am he, I am he who will sustain you. I have made you and I will carry you; I will sustain you and I will rescue you." Isaiah 46:3-4

Lord, as I look back over the years through all my pain and sorrow, I can see where you lifted me up in times of trouble. How your hand held onto me. How you carried me when I couldn't walk on my own. All the times I felt I was in a dry desert you were there. It is comforting to know that all I need to do is speak the name of Jesus and you surround me. Thank you Lord, I couldn't have made it without you.

"…I will not forget you! See, I have engraved you on the palms of my hands; your walls are ever before me." Isaiah 49:15-16

What a comfort Lord to know that you won't ever forget me; that all you have to do is turn your hand over and my name is engraved there. I must be really important to you Lord that you would engrave my name in the palm of your hand. I've never been that important to anyone. I've never had anyone love me like that. I'm so grateful that no matter what I do you won't forget me. I'll never be alone again. You see my obstacles, they are ever before me and you walk ahead of me and keep me safe. I love you too.

"I have put my words in your mouth and covered you with the shadow of my hand." Isaiah 51:16

Lord, let the words that I speak be your words, let them flow from me like a river and as they fall upon the ones listening, just like trees on a river bank, let them flourish and grow. I know Lord there have been many times in my life when I have walked in the shadow of your hand and it protected me. I don't know what I'd do without you Lord; my heart overflows with love for you.

"How beautiful on the mountains are the feet of those that bring good news, who proclaim peace, who bring good tidings, who proclaim salvation, who say to Zion your God reigns!"
Isaiah 52:7

Lord, I want my feet to bring good news to those who don't know you. I want my tongue to proclaim the peace that dwells within me when I rely on you. I want to proclaim your salvation from the mountains so all can hear. I want others to know that you reign. Let my feet not only bring good news, let them be good news so that wherever I walk Lord you are there and others will hear the good tidings I bring.

"For your Maker is your husband the Lord Almighty is his name the Holy One of Israel is your Redeemer, he is called the God of all the earth. The Lord will call you back as if you were a wife deserted and distressed in spirit a wife who married young...." Isaiah 54:5-6

When I was single Lord, I searched for my worth in men and my sin separated me from you. Father, it's my prayer that single women will look for worth and find it in you. That when they strive for a man to hold them they let that man be you and that for a time they discover what it is to have you be their husband, the head of their life. I pray that in their times of distress they feel your redemption and your love surround them like a blanket. I pray that they know Lord that they can sit in front of a fire, read your book and feel your fullness in their life. Physical touch will satisfy for an instant, but your touch will satisfy for a lifetime. Physical touch will only fill them with regret, but your touch will fill them to overflowing. I pray today Lord that you would touch all those yearning for a physical man with the anointing and touch of the Holy Spirit, and they will know what true love really is.

"The Lord will guide you always; he will satisfy your needs in a sun-scorched land and will strengthen your frame. You will be like a well-watered garden, like a spring whose waters never fail." Isaiah 58:11

Sometimes Lord I forget that all I need to do is listen and you will guide me. When my days seem like I can't take another step, I can call on you and you will strengthen me. I can eat your Word and listen quietly to hear your voice and you will touch me like a withering plant thirsting for water and your touch will nourish me. Help me to remember Lord that I have a never-ending stream of water flowing through my life and it's you.

"Instead of shame my people will receive a double portion, and instead of disgrace they will rejoice in their inheritance; and so they will inherit a double portion in their land, and everlasting joy will be theirs. Isaiah 61:7

What a wonderful promise Lord, to know that all the shame I used to feel will be replaced with a double portion from you and that instead of disgrace for my past, I have become an heir to your throne. I am royalty because I'm your daughter. I'm a princess and you are my king. I will walk the streets of gold with you and I'll never be poor again. My joy will overflow as I hold your hand and take in your kingdom. It's my prayer today Lord that whoever is reading this will know that if they belong to you, their Father is a king. That by accepting your grace they too can hold your hand and walk the streets of heaven someday.

"In you, Oh Lord, I have taken refuge; let me never be put to shame; deliver me in your righteousness." Psalm 31:1

Have years of doing the wrong thing brought shame to your heart? Jesus will wipe the shame away and put a new song in your heart. Even though you are full of sadness, do not give up; although Jesus seems far away, he is right beside you, loving you. Stand with your shoulders back and your head high because his blood has set you free and it covers you. You belong to Jesus, he is your Lord; climb into his lap let his arms surround you, feel his love embrace you. When the enemy reminds you of your past, remind him that you were made in the image of Jesus, his worst nightmare, and he can only take you as far as your knees.

"Be still before the Lord and wait patiently for him; do not fret when men succeed in their ways, when they carry out their wicked schemes." Psalm 37:7

Do you look around you and everyone else's life seems to be more wonderful than yours? Do you wonder how you got to this place of pain and sorrow? Do you look for your worth in men and find it's not there? Jesus is here, can you hear his voice? It's in the wind outside your door, it's in the sun shining through your window; it's in the flowers. He's talking to you and wanting to touch your heart in special places; listen and wait patiently for his timing is not yours. Rest in his arms while you wait and remember he loves you. Be quiet and listen, you will hear his voice; put your fear behind you for he is in every beautiful thing you see. Evil may seem to thrive, but in the end the beauty of the Lord will shine through.

"Commit your way to the Lord; trust him and he will do this:" Psalm 37:5

Are you struggling today and your marriage isn't what you dreamed it would be? He will change your husband's heart. Trust him and do not doubt. Be the woman he created you to be, show your husband love. Be Christ to him for by the acts of your heart he will see Jesus and know there is none other. Even in the midst of turmoil Jesus will take your hand; instead of rocks and weeds you will see fields of daisies blowing in the wind, you will feel the fresh breath of the Holy Spirit upon your life. Commit your way to the Lord and he will give you all you need. Let his countenance be upon you, let it shine from your face so that when you pass by, the light of the Lord will call to others and they will see by your life that you are HIS.

"For evil men will be cut off but those who hope in the Lord will inherit the land." Psalm 37:9

Be patient, trust in him for he has given you promises and he will fulfill them. We have hope in him and without it we will allow all the weaknesses of life to overtake us. Find joy in the midst of the storm and know that joy is Jesus. We have an inheritance; we are heirs to a throne. If you know that you are royalty, how can you not have hope? Share the joy so that others might know it too. I pray that all of heaven will be full of people who thought there was no hope and then HOPE rose up inside of them. He has called you to a mission to help others get to know him. He doesn't want us to go alone, he wants us to come and bring our neighbors and the lost with us. Share your hope! Show others how peace surrounds you, how in the midst of turmoil and trials you have JOY and they will inherit the land.

"If the Lord delights in a man's way, he makes his steps firm; though he stumble, he will not fall, for the Lord upholds him with his hand." Psalm 37:23

Hold fast to the cross and don't look for your worth in men. Know you are worthy because you are a child of the king. Although you feel lonely, you are not alone. Jesus is within you, he walks beside you, and He fills you with the Holy Spirit, you are His child. He is your safety net, the one who catches you when you fall. Don't let fear overtake you, don't believe the lies of the enemy. Jesus is the truth. Hang on to his truth and he will bring you through.

"Turn from evil and do good; then you will dwell in the land forever. For the Lord loves the just and will not forsake his faithful ones." Psalm 37:27-28

Do you feel like everywhere you turn there is evil? Does it seem like every thought you think is bad? Do not listen to the enemy; do not let him convince you with his lies, stay focused on Jesus for He is your strength. Keep your eyes on Him, fill your heart with His word, and know He loves you. You need no other but Him, for He alone will make you whole.

"I waited patiently for the Lord; he turned to me and heard my cry." Psalm 40:1

There are days Lord when I wonder where you are. Days when I feel all alone and no one cares, days when I have no sense of direction, and then I cry out to you and I feel your presence and I know that I am not alone. Thank you for hearing my cry; for helping me know that even in my times of despair you are always there.

"I do not hide your righteousness in my heart; I speak of your faithfulness and salvation...." Psalm 40:10

I don't ever want to forget where I came from and how worthless I felt before I found you. I want you to fill me Lord and as I feel your love rise up in me, let it flow from my lips that I might speak of your faithfulness. I want to dance before you and feel your love surround me. I want others to know you and feel the joy that you bring. Use me Lord today to make a difference.

"Though I walk in the midst of trouble, you preserve my life, you stretch out your hand against the anger of my foes, with your right hand you save me." Psalm 138:7

Don't put limitations on Jesus by doubting, for nothing can overpower you if you stay focused on him. Don't listen to what others say, only hear his voice. He will guide you in the way you should go. When you don't know what to do, be still and he will show you.

"Let the morning bring me word of your unfailing love, for I have put my trust in you. Show me the way I should go, for to you I lift up my soul. Rescue me from my enemies, O Lord, for I hide myself in you. Teach me to do your will, for you are my God; may your good Spirit lead me on level ground."
Psalm 143:8-10

Jesus is your hiding place, your shelter. Take what he has shown you to others so that they too know their worth is in his eyes and no other. Remember the enemy has no weapons, you are equipped for battle by the shed blood of Jesus; you have the power to overtake the enemy. Show others Jesus and speak to them of how only he can deliver them. Let them know that they should set their eyes and hearts on him and he will heal their wounded hearts. He will hear their cry of pain; only he can set them free from bondage.

"Praise be to the Lord my Rock, who trains my hands for war, my fingers for battle." Psalm 144:1

Jesus has great plans for you. He has a purpose for your life beyond your wildest dreams. Forget your past, all the lost hopes and dreams they are behind you. He will train your hands and your mind. He will make a way. You have God potential. He will anoint your hands and as you push forward, he will be your shield against the enemy. Focus on Jesus for he is with you now and until the end of time. Lay your burdens at his feet; let them go and only focus on him. He is the great I AM. Stand up! Hold firm, he's going to bless you!

"The Lord is gracious and compassionate; slow to anger and rich in love. The Lord is good to all; he has compassion on all he has made. All you have made will praise you, O Lord; your saints will extol you. They will tell of the glory of your kingdom and speak of your might....." Psalm 145:8-11

He has brought you to this place; use the wisdom He has given you to turn other hearts and eyes to Him. You are a woman of stature and strength; he made you and formed you. Even in your pain show others Jesus; even though they hurt he is the rock, the Almighty One. Through your pain, he will birth in you a mighty nation. Stand in the river's flow and feel the power of the Lord fill your veins. Exalt his holy name; speak of his glory and what he has done for you. Even though you hurt, his love surrounds you, and others will see and know Jesus is the one they are looking for.

"The Lord is righteous in all his ways and loving toward all he has made, the Lord is near to all who call on him, to all who call on him in truth, He fulfills the desires of those who fear him; he hears their cry and saves them. The Lord watches over all who love him, but all the wicked he will destroy." Psalm 145:17-20

Cast your eyes upon the beauty around you; listen for his voice in the whisper of the wind. He loves you with a love that is greater than any love you could ever imagine. You can climb into his lap and he will listen. He wants to hear your every dream, for you are his little girl. When you question and do not know which way to turn, stop and listen, for he will speak to you and show you the way in which to go. Stay true to his word and you shall have the desires of your heart.

"........The Lord sets prisoners free, the Lord gives sight to the blind, the Lord lifts up those who are bowed down, the Lord loves the righteous." Psalm 146: 7-8

Are you a prisoner to the world around you? Jesus can open your eyes and plant his word on the pages of your heart. If you think you are worthless, he can show you worth. If you walk with a slump, stand tall, throw your shoulders back and hold your head high. You are an heir to a throne; you are a princess to a King. Change your ways; keep your feet on his path, firmly planted in the soil of the cross. See his face, know his love surrounds you and keeps you from harm. Jesus is all things, you are worthy in his eyes, he will not forsake you. He is calling you to battle against the enemy to show people his love. Help set his people free.

"May the praise of God be in their mouths and a double-edged sword in their hands." Psalm 149:6

Do you know that Jesus heals the broken hearted? If your heart is broken, stand in faith believing and Jesus will mend it. Be joyful in the Lord for he will sustain you in your sadness. Celebrate the living God. From this day forth, walk as he walked, love as he loved, be humble; do not put yourself above others, take time to love all you see with the love of Christ. Speak his name and he is there, he holds you up and some day you will see his face and his holiness will surround you.

"Praise the Lord. Praise God in his sanctuary; praise him in his mighty heavens. Praise him for his acts of power, praise him for his surpassing greatness. Praise him with the sounding of the trumpet, praise him with the harp and lyre, praise him with tambourine and dancing, praise him with the strings and flute, praise him with the clash of cymbals, praise him with resounding cymbals. Let everything that has breath, praise the Lord." Psalm 150

Walk with Jesus and in your trials he will lift you up. He has given you wisdom, discernment and understanding; do not grow faint for he is always with you. He will keep his promises, for when he speaks it is truth. In all your ways honor him and when you speak his name; people will see him in your face and life. You are his daughter, full of the love of Christ. He will never forsake you or leave you. Do not worry for he will supply your every need. Walk in faith with the love of Christ that is beyond all human understanding, and your heart will fill up with love for him, and his truth will flow from your lips.

"For you created my inmost being; you knit me together in my mother's womb. I praise you because I am fearfully and wonderfully made; your works are wonderful, I know that full well." Psalm 139:13-14

Isn't Jesus awesome? You are unique, one of a kind. You are precious to him, a jewel in his treasure chest and when he holds you in his hand and his light shines on you, you are full of dazzling color, a rainbow in the lives of others. When Jesus formed you he had great things in mind for you. Jesus had called you long before you knew. He called you before you were made and through your pain he formed you and made you wise. You are a precious woman full of wisdom and because he loves you, he will hold you up and you will not fall. He will cover your children and they too shall know him.

"Set a guard over my mouth, O Lord; keep watch over the door of my lips." Psalm 141:3

Lord, there are days when I feel like I need a muzzle on my mouth, days when I feel like everything I speak comes out to bite and hurt. In your infinite wisdom Lord help me to speak only truth; do not let the words of my mouth slander anyone, for I know that in speaking the truth with love, I will show them Jesus. Others will see you in me and know I belong to you. I will praise your name today, the name of Jesus, even if I'm feeling weary and you will hold me up.

"....I will pour out my Spirit on your offspring, and my blessing on your descendants. They will spring up like grass in a meadow, like poplar trees by flowing streams." Isaiah 44:3-4

Lord, there are days when I feel so much regret about how I was as a mother. There are times when I want to go back and make everything right. I could have done so much better. Thank you for this scripture. And for letting me know that even though I wasn't the best mother, you can still save my children and touch their hearts. Thank you for allowing me to become a blessing to my children, to show them Jesus in my life and allow you working through me to erase some of the pain I caused them. I know Lord by your promise, that if I allow them to see you in me and as they see love and understanding in my heart, they will grow to love and thirst after you and you will set them free. I know that as I grow in knowledge of you and your word and as I allow you to fill me with your Holy Spirit, love will flow out of me and touch their hearts. You are my fuel Jesus, my bread of life.

"I will go before you and will level the mountains; I will break down gates of bronze and cut through bars of iron." I will give you the treasures of darkness, riches stored in secret places, so that you may know that I am the Lord." Isaiah 45:2-3

Jesus will go before you and break down the walls of iron. Mountains will not stand in your way, for he will clear a path for you so that you might walk in the anointing; and as you open your mouth the words of God will flow from your lips. He is the God who made all things and none can come against him and succeed. He has come to set you free from the enemy. If you ask him; he will open doors and he will make a path for you. Do not turn from him, for when you do, you grow weary and lose your focus. Look up, he is there!

"…..I summon you by name and bestow on you a title of honor, though you do not acknowledge me. I am the Lord, there is no other, apart from me there is no God. I will strengthen you, though you have not acknowledged me, so that from the rising of the sun to the place of its setting men may know there is none besides me. I am the Lord, and there is no other. I form the light and create darkness, I bring prosperity and create disaster; I, the Lord, do these things."
Isaiah 45:4-7

It amazes me to think that Jesus knows my name and he has written it on the palm of his hand. My past is behind me and I need not be ashamed, for he has formed me and I am his daughter. He has given me stature and grace. He has allowed me to see into the dark places of my life and through the pain I've come out into the light. He's taken my ugliness and turned it into beauty. Not the kind of superficial beauty that someone sees on the outside, but the inner beauty that shines like a light from my face; a beauty that doesn't fade with age, but continues to the grave. My worth is in him and I have nothing to fear.

"O Lord, I say to you, "You are my God," Hear, O Lord, my cry for mercy." Psalm 140:6

Keep your eyes on Jesus, fill your heart with his word; know in your heart that he loves you, and you need no other but him; he alone will make you whole. Although there are times when you feel lonely, remember you are not alone, Jesus is within you; he walks beside you, he fills you with his Holy Spirit and you are his child. You are full of wisdom, compassion, understanding and love. Show these things to all you see and they will see Jesus in you. You will shine and they will know it is God who is your strength.

"…I will make breath enter you and you will come to life."
Ezekiel 37:5

Thank you Lord that in my time of desperation you were there and you breathed life into me. I am so grateful that you love me that much. What was dead is now gone and my life has meaning and a purpose. I give this day to you to do with as you will. I love you.

"When I consider your heavens, the work of your fingers, the moon and the stars, which you have set in place, what is man that you are mindful of him, the son of man that you care for him?" Psalm 8:3-4

Lord, I think about how in the vast universe I am but a speck and you are mindful of me and it takes my breath away. Lord, you made the heavens and the earth and set them all in place. How great and awesome you are. Thank you for being my friend. Thank you for opening my eyes that I might see you better. Thank you that you never gave up on me. May I always walk being mindful of you and your great love for me.

"let us draw near to God with a sincere heart in full assurance of faith, having our hearts sprinkled to cleanse us from a guilty conscience and having our bodies washed with pure water." Hebrews 10:22

Lord on the day I came to you and gave you my life, I stood at the foot of the cross and you sprinkled your blood on my heart and cleansed me from all my guilt and shame. As the blood dripped from your crown of thorns, it dropped on my heart and made it clean. Clean, everything gone, white as snow. Sometimes I wonder how you could love me that much, that you would wipe all my sins away. Help me to always be mindful Lord of how you love me, so that when the enemy tries to remind me of my past, I can remind him of his future. Thank you for never giving up on me, I am forever grateful.

"Be self-controlled and alert. Your enemy the devil prowls around like a roaring lion looking for someone to devour. Resist him, standing firm in the faith, because you know that your brothers throughout the world are undergoing the same kind of sufferings." 1 Peter 5:8-9

Lord, as I apply the blood of Jesus to my life; be with me and protect me from the one who wants to take my life away. Let the enemy be far away from me as I walk in the confidence that you protect me. Let me be ever mindful that the enemy is roaming the earth wanting to devour those that follow you, so that I can stand firm in my Savior and pray for those around the world that are fighting the same battle. Thank you for another day to walk with you.

"...Everyone should be quick to listen, slow to speak and slow to become angry, for man's anger does not bring about the righteous life that God desires." James 1:19-20

Today Lord let me be slow to speak and quick to listen; let me hear the cries of those who are hurting and have a compassionate heart. Help me to know Lord when my anger is righteous and when it is hurtful and depart from it. I want to become all that you desire me to be. As I open my ears to listen, give me wisdom and understanding of the pain that others feel; then when I open my mouth to speak, out of my heart will flow compassion and love rather than condemnation and anger.

"For the word of God is living and active. Sharper than any double-edged sword, it penetrates even to dividing soul and spirit, joints and marrow; it judges the thought and attitudes of the heart." Hebrews 4:12

Lord, today let your word be alive in me and as I read it, stamp it on my heart so that I might have a well-spring of your word within me. Show me in your word what you want me to know and let it flow to the marrow of my bones. As I read, let the attitude of my heart be the same attitude that you have, so that I might look at those around me in need and they will see Jesus in me. Let your word cut out the thoughts and attitudes of my heart that are not of you so that I might be a witness of your love and grace today.

54

"Then you will call, and the Lord will answer; you will cry for help, and he will say: Here I am...." Isaiah 58:9

Thank you Lord that I am never by myself, that you are always here and that when I cry out to you, you will answer and hear my cry for help. It's so comforting to know that I am never alone, that you are always with me. Thank you Lord that in the quiet times when I sit early in the morning you reassure me by whispering to my heart: "Here I am: I love you, you're my daughter and I will always be here for you."

"The Spirit of the Sovereign Lord is on me, because the Lord has anointed me to preach good news to the poor. He has sent me to bind up the brokenhearted, to proclaim freedom for the captives and release from darkness for the prisoners...."
Isaiah 61:1

I look back at my life and all the mistakes that I've made and I stand in awe that you would anoint someone like me to spread the good news to those who are hurting and have no hope. I am so grateful Lord that you saw something in me when the world only saw mistakes and failures. Thank you for allowing me to take those mistakes and failures and use them to show others hope in a God that never fails. I am forever yours.

"The nations will see your righteousness, and all kings your glory; you will be called by a new name that the mouth of the Lord will bestow." Isaiah 62:2

I wonder sometimes Lord what my new name will be. On that day when you open your mouth to speak what you'll call me. Will I have lived my life walking with you daily, learning all about you? Will I touch lives the way you did? Will your love flow from me and touch others? Will what breaks your heart break mine? I so want to be like you Lord; I want to walk like you, touch others' lives like you, and I want what breaks your heart to break mine, so that someday the name you give me will be "She Loved Well."

"You have made known to me the path of life; you will fill me with joy in your presence, with eternal pleasures at your right hand." Psalm 16:11

Thank you Lord for filling me with joy and showing me that life is a journey toward being more like you. As I am other centered I have joy even in the midst of troubled times. As I strive daily to be more like you Lord, surround me with your love, let it flow from me like a river. When I open my mouth to speak, let it be your words. Fill me so that others might see you in my face. Help me to live my life with you in mind knowing that at the end of my life there are eternal pleasures from the hand of God waiting for me.

"Show the wonder of your great love, you who save by your right hand those who take refuge in you from their foes. Keep me as the apple of your eye; hide me in the shadow of your wings." Psalm 17:7-8

It's hard to believe sometimes Lord that I could be the apple of your eye. That you delight in me and are concerned for me. At those times in my life when I thought no one cared, you did. You believed in me when I couldn't even believe in myself. How could you love me that much? I'm so grateful that you do and that I can crawl into your lap and hide in the shadow of your wings when the world gets to be more than I can bear. Thank you for always being there, for never giving up on me, for showing me what true love really looks like. I love you.

"You, O Lord, keep my lamp burning; my God turns my darkness into light. With your help I can advance against a troop; with my God I can scale a wall." Psalm 18:28-29

Lord, as I come before you this morning I think about the times that you turned my darkness into light. The many ways that you have shown me how to scale a wall and helped me to know that with you I can do anything. I am amazed by how much you love me, how you are always there to lift me up. Thank you for being my shield and strength and for never giving up on me. I give this day to you Lord; help me to be a blessing to someone today.

"The King is enthralled by your beauty; honor him, for he is your lord." Psalm 45:11

Deep down, we all want to know we're beautiful. How can you love me so much? I've made so many mistakes in my life; I don't know how you can be enthralled with my beauty Lord when there are days that I don't come close to feeling beautiful. I thank you that I'm an imperfect vessel, a clay pot with cracks; and when I'm filled with living water it seeps out through my cracks and waters the things in its path and they become a thing of beauty, not because of anything I've done. It's all because of you.

"Be still, and know that I am God;...." Psalm 46:10

Stop your busyness, and sit with me for a while and know that I am here; you can see me, you can hear me if you're silent. I'm all around you, in a new born baby, flowers in the spring. Sit just for a while, lay your head in my lap and let me stroke your hair. Let me fill you, refresh you, touch you. After you've sat with me, you can look into their eyes and see the sadness there; you can give them hope and help them to know they are not alone. Touch their pain and help me change their sadness into joy. You can't do it alone. When the sun breaks through the dawn, sit at my feet and let me love you.

My Story

As a young woman growing up my life at home left a lot to be desired, I had a father who didn't know how to show me love, so as a young woman I started looking for love in all the wrong places. Physical touch became love to me because I didn't know the true meaning of intimacy. Every time I was physical with a man, I lost a part of myself. I endured physical and emotional pain because I thought that is what I deserved. I lost the kind of relationships I could have had with my children because I was wanting love so desperately myself.

I saw myself as ugly all my life and that ugliness followed me into womanhood. Because of my poor self-image, I had no confidence in myself. I looked for men to fill my needs and when I did that, I gave them the place in my life where God should have been. I wanted the ideal man who would fill the void, someone who would never hurt me. The truth is, there is no mortal man who can do that.

My story is not so unlike that of the woman at the well. Because of my poor self-image and no role model to show me how to do healthy relationships, I had several failed marriages. I lost most of my life because I kept making the wrong choices. Not until I was willing to break free of my past and look at the truth about myself and why I made poor choices did I stop losing.

When all seemed lost, an amazing thing happened. I found hope in God and I realized that my hope was secure even if my life was not. When I quit insisting that life go my way and put aside my agenda and invited God to do whatever he wanted with my life; that was the beginning.

Now my self-assurance comes from living to please God, not people. When I stopped looking to others to validate my life, I didn't have to depend on what they thought to make me feel ok about myself. When I realized that God loves me just the way I am, I could stop running and turn toward him. This encounter with true love fills me to the depth of my being. As I learned to rely on God and His love, human relationships no longer are a desperate attempt to find someone to love me perfectly. Instead, God fills me up. His love springs up inside of me and overflows to others and I can offer living water to those who hurt like I did. I am no longer ugly, but beautiful, and it has nothing to do with my looks but it has everything to do with my heart.

I have lost a lot but what I've found is far greater than all the losses. God has covered me with his blood and has allowed me to use my mistakes to minister to others and understand the pain and hurt they feel because I've been there. What an awesome privilege for me to serve Him and others and how it blesses my life when God's glory shines through, not because of something I've done; but because of what He can do through me and someone He has placed in my path sees themselves as beautiful too. He took this woman who thought she was worthless and made me into a worthy woman who loves God and I am forever grateful.

It is my hope as you read through the pages of this book that Jesus touched you in the depth of your heart and where you are wounded he began to set you free and you will begin to see with the eyes of your heart that you are a precious jewel with many facets; and as He continues to heal your heart, like a diamond you will sparkle and shine with the love of Christ.

CPSIA information can be obtained
at www.ICGtesting.com
Printed in the USA
FSOW02n1836280916
25516FS

9 781434 342270